HIGH PROFITS IN **FLIPPING HOUSES**

How To Make High Profits Buying and Selling Houses In Your Local Market

"Hidden Deals Are Everywhere...You Just Have To Know Where To Find Them."

Copyright © 2018.
All Rights Reserved

Published By:

14837 Detroit Avenue
Suite 202
Lakewood, Ohio 44107

(216) 220-7027
www.ValleyWideInvestments.com

Disclaimer:

Information contained in this guide is for educational purposes. Always verify information against your local laws and conditions. During the investment property buying process, it is wise to have professional legal help of an attorney skilled in real estate law local to the property. This guide is not meant to take the place of professional one-to-one advice, but only to complement such advice. The information in this guide is the opinion of the author. Income and profit examples in this book are unique to the writer, and are not indicative of what the reader will achieve using information in this book. In other words, do not blame me if you make a bad purchase or run your property into the ground because you don't know how to run a business.

Please Note: Information contained in this guide is for educational purposes. Always verify information against your local laws and conditions. During the investment property buying process, it is wise to have professional legal help of an attorney skilled in real estate law local to the property. This guide is not meant to take the place of professional one-to-one advice, but only to complement such advice. The information in this guide is the opinion of the author.

Income Disclaimer: Examples of profit or income in this book are unique to the author only and are not meant to serve as what the Reader will earn in real estate. Please do your own due diligence in real estate investing; as in any business there is the risk that you may have a loss or gain.

Table of Contents

Introduction 1

Chapter 1: My Quick Story 5

Chapter 2: How It Works... 15

Chapter 3: Why Hot Markets? 31

Chapter 4: How To Find Hidden Deals In Hot Areas 34

INTRODUCTION

"This Book Will Show You How To Quick-Flip Homes With High Profit Margins In Any Market"

Be A BIG Fish In A Small (Real Estate) Pond – It Works!

Flipping Houses Is a Real Proven Avenue To Wealth Creation – And It Can Happen Really Fast

How Can I Say This?

...Because I have tried many avenues in real estate investing; and flipping wholesale properties for "quick" cash profits is the easiest and most hassle-free way to go.

I have built rental portfolios, flipped apartments, flipped retail houses, wore the contractor management hats, and flipped hundreds of cash flow rental income properties in Cleveland. The best money maker was always wholesaling GOOD PROFITABLE DEALS FOR ALL PARTIES INVOLVED to cash investors/buyers, yielding a very liquid cash business FOR OVER 13 YEARS and even in the middle of the infamous "Housing Crash" of 2008-2013.

WAIT, before you say that it only worked because of all the cheap deals back then, you need to know I started BEFORE the Housing Crash and it still worked, and AFTER the Crash all the way up to now in 2018. People make money in real estate in all markets, if you have trouble believing that, then it is going to hold you back for sure.

Wholesaling properties to cash buyers' works really well in a Sellers' market or heated economy, because you don't need to search for buyers, they are everywhere; it's a 10:1 Buyer-to-good-deal ratio. The only thing you have to focus on is strategic marketing and networking to find bargain deals in your particular market or "backyard."

This mini-book can show you how to find, create and farm a little niche in your local market that can NET you a profit of $60,000 to $250,000 per year with very little work, and only about 5-10 hours a week. I can say this with confidence because I have been doing it for over 13 years in 2-3 zip codes of Cleveland, Ohio, that's a long time. Of course you can do much but that's where you start losing time freedom.

Also, please don't think that you cannot do this in your market, because you think there are no good deals there. They're there they just don't transact on the MLS, foreclosure auction or consumer websites like Zillow or FSBO websites. Go beyond traditional channels and use your brain; you have to go to the deals first before they get to the marketplace. **Sound like hard work? IT IS!** But guess what, any real estate investor that is successful has to work HARD, and this is no different than anything else, it will take time to develop and reap revenues. So with that being said, let's move on.

So, once again, this system works great in Sellers' market; When you are flipping in a hot market, the main major goal is to find a great deal. Buyers are automatically there. Dealing only with property and sellers can be a lot easier than meeting and finding buyers that may not meet your criteria or waste your time. This may sound counter-intuitive but allow me to explain through-out this guide.

I believe from experience that the #1 goal in real estate investing or flipping is to find and develop niches. Once you find a good niche, farm the hell out of it and keep it going as long as it works. When it dies, develop another one, and so forth. This strategy has worked for me since 2003-2004 when I ventured into real estate investing part-time while still working a full time job as a Police Officer in Cleveland.

I'm going to show you why finding great deals in a hot Sellers' market neighborhood is easier than finding or marketing for qualified and/or cash buyers.

Also, you will be selling to cash rehabbers and homeowners only. You won't be selling to cash flow investors or financed investors, and I will show you why that is even better for you in making bigger and faster profits.

This is a great little business that can be scaled up to $1 million with some work, but is better run at a $150,000 to $250,000 revenue level as that will give you the most FREEDOM and 80/20 effect to your life.

"Smallness (80/20 principal application), liquidity in deals and velocity are the 3 components to success with this small boutique cash machine anyone can set up anywhere in or near a large city in the United States."

CHAPTER 1

MY QUICK STORY

Who Am I And What Value Can I Offer You?

I am a real estate investor, flipper and re-developer in Cleveland doing this full time. I have flipped over 351 homes and apartments since 2004. I know that's not a lot for almost 15 years, but I achieve huge margins for what is invested and that's where I think my strategies may have some value for you.

Over the years I discovered the best 80/20 strategies for achieving wealth in real estate flipping, building huge cash reserves, and being FREE while running a real estate flipping business. I also learned how to leverage the Internet to automate this process so that I can really be anywhere I want, China, Mexico, Belize, Vancouver, Amsterdam, San Diego..you name it.

Freedom and hassle-free net profits is the best way to go in the real estate investing business.

How I Started..

I was 26 years old when I started a part-time real estate flipping business in my brother's finished attic in Cleveland, Ohio. It was a 7 x 10 foot room and was very hot in the summer. I was broke, living on $30,000 a year and ready for a change. That was over 14 years ago and this little niche flipping enterprise has grossed millions in profits, JUST in 2 ZIP CODES of Cleveland!

Wholesale flips were how I started. Why? Because I decided that I wanted all of the profit now instead over a long period of time, after analyzing other investors in the marketplace that were very bad at managing rentals or were buying them with LOTS of mortgage leverage. I don't mind paying the short term cap gains, and I'll tell you why later.

So in this very simple, niche house flipping business I will describe here is very real and works; and requires very little time once you get it set up. The only difference is now you will rely on mostly internet technologies, whereas when is started I was initially relying on direct mail, visits to the courthouse and newspaper marketing strategies, more about this later too.

You also need a source of cash available to buy. My systems are based on cash purchases, and not creative terms or other no cash down techniques. With the amount of available PRIVATE wealth out there, this should not be a major hurdle for new investors. It was how I started and private lenders are in almost every city of America, you can find them anywhere, it is not a difficult task.

If you don't think you can find a private lender to work with you, it is a personal belief problem you have to solve.

In 2004 I was a 6-year full time police officer in Cleveland. I was sick and tired of the low pay and life-draining departmental politics, I began reading books on my downtime about real estate investing and short sales while at work.

My vague goal at the time was to find a way to massively replace my income and be free from being a police officer. Although I was highly motivated when I entered law enforcement, I realized pretty fast that there was no real future...for me at least, financially or career-oriented. I remember officers retiring that could not afford the Public Retirement health insurance to stay covered and had to take on part time jobs AFTER retirement just to pay it.

Dealing with the public and seeing and interacting with some of societies criminals and negative-minded individuals was not exactly something I wanted to do for the next 15 years at that point. Now don't get me wrong, I loved the police work (Especially traffic investigation), but it definitely took its toll and what was even more difficult was dealing with departmental politics and conflicts, like any other large organization.

I lived paycheck-to-paycheck like most Americans and was always about $500 from being broke. I had no assets or savings. I lived in a 2 bedroom side-by-side duplex in Cleveland's West side Kamms Corner neighborhood, where a lot of fireman and cops lived at that time.

So I began reading, following and applying strategies in the books and chose short sales as my first path. It was a struggle to force myself into action but I did it. Back then Bank One was still around and I figured out a way to "flip" wholesale properties at closing to cash rehabbers. These homes were Bank One pre-foreclosures.

My VERY FIRST cash PROFIT check on a flip (wholesale flip) was $10,300. Now this was a long time ago and things have changed a lot since then so this particular technique no longer works. But when I pulled this deal off I discovered my new passion and doorway to wealth and freedom. Those were exciting times and that's how it will be for any new investor when they get their first wholesale profit check.

I went on to do 20 more deals like this in 2005 until Bank One was bought by Chase and it would no longer work. Plus, banks starting making it mandatory that a Realtor was involved and that the property was listed on MLS for at least 3-6 months. So that was the end of my pre-foreclosures niche. YOU HAVE TO ADAPT EVEN IN REAL ESTATE INVESTING OR suffer the consequences.

When I started investing most areas were over-priced, it was near the real estate bubble/peak and it was hard to find good deals through traditional sources like MLS. The Internet was also way more archaic than now. In fact, in 2004 most people did not even know how to look property up online to see who owned it.

Foreclosure Crisis 2008

In 2005 some people talking about all of the exotic mortgages that investors were using, were going to implode in the next 3-5 years. Almost no one believed it. not even me. I didn't care because I was only working in the low-income areas which was the ONLY place to find distress real estate at good discounts for wholesale flips.

I wasn't using mortgages so I didn't care. All of my investor-buyers were cash buyers.

When 2007-2008 rolled around foreclosure property became extremely plentiful and cheap. It was the best time ever for cash investors. For the next 6 years it was so easy to get great deals, they were everywhere and they were quality deals. Most other mortgaged investors got burned, or became very scared. I kept going because my formulas for fast flips worked.

Sure there were a few times when the news outlets were really screaming "end of the world" and I felt like the only investor in my marketplace, in certain neighborhoods. Even the weekly Sheriff sale auction dwindled down to only 15-20 people for a brief period of time.

But my system kept working with very little effort in Cleveland, I even got to the point where I only was working 3-6 hours a week, and I still made at least $150,000 a year in net profits. And because almost all work was being done online at that point, I decided to move to Scottsdale, AZ and enjoy my freedom and sunshine.

When I moved to Scottsdale, the local County foreclosure trustee sales were selling 1990's-built stucco homes with pools for $55,000 to $85,000 that previously sold for $200,000 to $350,000. This was at the peak of the foreclosures in 2010-11. In hindsight, I don't think we will experience that again, in our lifetime.

I ended up living in Scottsdale for 5 years; it was hard to leave there. Most of my work was online and in attracting cash buyers, looking at potential deals and making offers (that was my system at the time). Since the Economy was presumably unstable, you would think it would be hard, but it wasn't that bad at all.

Some of the best years I had with the wholesale flipping business were when I lived in Phoenix and ran it from my desktop/laptop/mobile phone. I had perfected this business to yield a NET profit of $15,000 to $35,000 per WHOLESALE flip. Some needed absolutely zero work, some I would put $3,000 to $7,000 into it, but it was always cookie-cutter type of repairs. I had a small team on the ground (2 people), and it was very, very simple.

Once again, my main focus was buyer acquisition. The problem was, so many buyers were inexperienced and I had to educate a lot of people on items like how to fill out a contract, how to set up a utility account, how to turn on a utility, basically running their business for them. Not fun.

Many buyers would call me and want to be educated free for months. I realized then that dealing with MOTIVATED DISTRESSED PROPERTY SELLERS is SO much easier, and dealing with REO sellers is and was the best!! Some of you may remember, Fannie and Freddie were the best distressed sellers in the old days, they used to be so easy to get deals from, no deed restrictions, no First Look Period and fast fire-sale prices for cash buyers, simple!

Without getting into more details about my story, I ended up going into retail rehabs and developing rental portfolio properties for myself and other investors that wanted 10, 20 SFH's or duplexes, apartment buildings, etc.

When I strayed off the wholesale flipping business and life became much, MUCH more stressful and I lost a lot of my freedom

What I Learned From 10+ Years

Retail Rehabs and Rental Properties vs Wholesale Flipping

I decided to go deep into the retail rehabbing business in nice neighborhoods. I also wanted to build permanent rental portfolios for myself and others investors that wanted that.

My first rental goal was to buy and re-develop 15 duplexes fast in Cleveland the way I always get them. Simultaneously I would look for retail rehab homes to sell for top dollar to homeowners in certain trendy West side and East Side neighborhoods of Cleveland (Popular areas for city homeowners at the time, up to now)

Long Profits Vs Quick Profits

Real estate investing is one of those businesses ANYONE can do to generate large lump sums of cash fast, IF THEY BUY RIGHT, at an equitable price and in the right area.

The rentals brought in over six figures in net cash flow income for the 12 months, plus lots of real equity of course, since I bought them low, like I always do. I already knew the exact science needed to perfect the cash flow rental business since most of what I have done was flip income properties to investors.

Why I believe rentals won't make you RICH from cash flow? What I went through to establish and maintain the cash flow was life-draining. The biggest constraint were the property managers that constantly let me down; plus, I calculated the amount of net revenues make on a wholesale flip equals about 5-7 years of net rental income profit.

So, why wait 7 years when I can have it all now? There are tax liabilities incurred because of this though, but I'd rather pay the tax now and get my freedom, versus get the tax benefits of rentals but lose my freedom, does this make sense to you? What you go through to earn over 7 years in rental income you can make in 2-3 months, it comes out the same. I use 7 years because that is the average time an investor keeps a rental property in a dense market, based on my experiences.

I basically lost all of my freedom on the retail rehab business as well. They were GREAT deals in GREAT areas, but the contractors ran me into the ground and a variety of other ancillary effects wore me out. In fact, one of the rehabs was a major one and was so life-draining and difficult COMPARED to what I was used to, that I just decided to shut it all down in October of 2015 and figure out what I was doing wrong.

I figured out where the constraint was; Contractor Management and Deal Velocity.

Rehabilitating "retail" or high end homes is not for the unskilled or timid. Dealing with subs and contractors is a skill that some do not have and never will. There are other investors that are great with contractors and have the will-power to control them and constantly fire and rehire, or create an internal permanent crew.

I realized that it was not for me, because I like to be FREE and be able to move around a lot and that just won't happen in retail rehabbing or construction.

I went back and analyzed all the retail, higher-end rehabs I had performed since starting (about 45) . Every single one of them had a lower NET profit margin than the wholesale flips. Not only that, but it also brought back memories of stress, over budgets, completely incompetent trades and contractors, rip-offs, vandalism, "ripping-and-a-running", being the home depot Gopher, etc.

I can go on and on about all the bad. The only positive aspect I can pencil out is the feeling of satisfaction of remodeling a home to your special personal trademarks or providing a fully remodeled home to a new homeowner that loves it and gladly pay top dollar. It just feels good, but it wasn't enough for me to do more.

80/20 Principles

So I sat down and figured out what 20% inputs were giving me 80% of my best revenues. It was the quick wholesale flips. Pretty obvious now, I wanted a new niche, one where buyers would easily come to me, and the only thing I really had to do was find the deals and maybe deal with motivated sellers if it wasn't REO.

I did just that and it is a great niche to utilize when it's a Sellers' market! But it still works in a buyers' market, you just have to be in the absolutely best area that homeowners want to live, best rental deals or the young professionals type of neighborhoods.

The best part is that it is becoming a huge opportunity now because, in my opinion, the next wave in distress real estate is tax delinquency (foreclosures) and estate sales!

CHAPTER 2

HOW IT WORKS

How To Find The High Profit Deals In 2018+

The "SleeperDeals" Method
What is a SleeperDeal?

It's a great bargain no one knows about, is not on the MLS but you discover through one of the below creative marketing techniques. When you find and flip them, other investors will wonder how the hell you did that because it was never on the MLS or at Sheriff Sale.

It's also a way of describing the HUGE amount of homes out there sitting there waiting for a motivated investor like you to come along and wake them up to sell to you.

When distressed owners are in trouble, they often freeze up and don't know what to do or who to trust. You want your name in front of them somehow.

Direct Mail

This activity alone has generated so much revenue for my company in the past 10 years. It is a sure-fire way to find deals, and it works in huge markets too, but with smaller response rates. Direct mail is a system that will start working 1-3 months after you start, and keep working as long as you keep mailing. I just did a 30 piece mailing in Cleveland in a certain zip code and it generated one deal with a $15,000 net profit potential. The ROI is insane on specialized targeted real estate mailing campaigns.

It is a great method that will fill your pipeline for as long as you keep sending out letters or postcards. One deal can give you the funds to direct mail for the next 5 years. You will discover that your R.O.I. on direct mail costs is huge when flipping wholesale property.

What's great about local direct mail is that out of a 1,000 – 2,000 unit mailing, it will often yield some really good leads in which you can get 1-2 good profit deals out of that one mailing, but testing is key to getting that number higher with less units mailed.

I generally get at least 1-2 deals out of a 1,000 unit mailing, especially letters as they are opened and taken more seriously. The obstacle many investors run into is that they lose their marketing momentum and stop sending out mail once they get a deal, or they don't have a targeted list. The list is very important, if you are sending mail to owners that are not motivated; your chances of getting a GOOD DEAL are low. You will get owners calling you for sure, but they will want full price or just not be motivated. You want to avoid this because you will lose money and motivation in your marketing expenditures.

Your profit is always in your buy price, most other parameters are controllable, such as construction labor, material sources, costs, renal processes, selling price, etc. If you don't get a good buy price then you will lose money in real estate.

How Do You Find a Targeted List?

Core Logic / ListSource.com (Most reliable but expensive)

One of the largest data brokers for property and other databases. They are usually connected to the county data servers, but there is a lag in the time it takes for their database to populate the nationwide county database updates. They require you to subscribe or buy property record leads. They can be quite expensive. I would only use them if I have allocated a large budget for property mailings .. usually over $15,000.

General List Vendors

There are lots to choose from, but I recommend CoreLogic if you have the budget, they have been the most accurate with my mailings.

USPS

Getting a list of vacant homes is really only available from the US Postal service. Many list vendors will say they have vacant homes data, but they really are just absentee owners with out of state or difference tax mailing addresses recorded.

The USPS has a requirement that you be a non-profit in order to get the actual vacant homes data. Actual vacant property data lists can be hard to generate because a person has to physically verify that it is vacant, and returned mail is usually performed by the postal service.

County Direct

You could approach the county you are in directly and ask for special mailings, sometimes they charge you but at least you'll know it is raw data and as accurate as possible. When you contact the county auditor's office, try to speak with the I.T. department because usually they are the ones that deal with property records, and if you are blessed they may give you the direct log in to their public FTP website where you can download any kind of property criteria you are looking for at anytime.

Real Estate Brokers

Most real estate agents and brokers have access to the tax records in the MLS interface and can generate lists, but often this data is a little behind in accuracy unfortunately.

Another way to determine vacant homes is by driving around neighborhoods. This always works in any market.

Who do you send mail to?

- Tax delinquent owners (pending or filed tax lien property)
- Vacant property
- Free and clear, mortgage-free owners
- Out-of-town owners (Have an out of state tax mailing address)
- Estate/probate property
- Attorneys / financial professionals / insurance agents

All of these parameters can be narrowed down in your list vendor, or we can make you custom reports at FindForeclosure.net for Cuyahoga County.

How Do You Send Out Mail?

Farm a zip code or neighborhood – Focusing in on niche neighborhoods will bring you the fastest deals. For instance, when is started in 2004, I focused on the 44105 zip code of Cleveland because there were A LOT of cheap deals to be had there. I then moved into the 44120 zip code areas, then 44129 of Parma..and I acquired many pre-foreclosures in Parma from BankOne as a result of my letters to defaulted mortgage filings (Which I had to manually record out of the legal newspaper everyday)

Today I have 10 zip codes in 2 states that I "farm" that bring me consistent deals. These deals are SELDOM ever on the MLS and are almost always low mortgages or no mortgages. Consistently sending letters will keep your pipeline full of profitable deal flow.

FYI, even back in 2004 very few other investors were doing this, I think there were like 2-3 out of the whole area that were sending out letters too, I know this because I would always ask a seller if they received any other letters from investors and if so, what made them call me, <u>their response was always the same; I picked up my phone when the called or called them back the fastest</u>.

Split Testing Letters

Use different copyrights formats to see which letter works best. This is age-old marketing routines, you split test different ad marketing copies to see which one works for what list. Since direct mail is a long term strategy, you should do this; because when you do find a super converting letter, you can scale up and do a larger targeted mailing for tremendously positive results. Split testing can take up to 3-6 months, but it's worth it.

Blanket Mailing Routes or Whole Neighborhoods

Sometimes sending a postcard to every residential home in a particular niche neighborhood can yield long term results. I have tried this with the USPS's EveryDoor Direct Mail program. It is a low cost blanket mailing, you define what route you want to mail to and bundle up the letters or postcards and take them to the postal office.

It's cheap, and will work over a period of time, but you will get a lot of unmotivated seller calls. But, many owners will save your postcard or letter and then call you when they suddenly have to sell fast and don't have time to mess with a real estate agent

Streets of Gold

Forget the term appearance; this method has yielded great deals for me. When I drive, and see a property that gives off a subtle clue, I know there is some form of distress very possible with that house. I follow up by researching title, owner and mortgage status.. if any, the same day.

Subtle clues to look for:

- Lawn is not maintained
- Newspapers everywhere
- Mailbox full
- Posted letter on door or window
- Debris in yard, unkempt lawn.
- Window drapes all open, or no drapes at all.
- No activity for a while.
- No cars ever in driveway
- Looks like it needs repairs.
- No lights on at night
- LOOKS EMPTY.
- Follow your hunches.

What's strange is that once you get a few deals this way you get a good ability at "sensing" a "hidden" deal when you see one. I don't have the words to explain it, you just know, only investors that have done this will understand.

Internet Marketing

All eyeballs are on the Internet now. When I check my web stats, around 82% of all internet visitors to my websites are using a tablet or smart phone. That is huge and only going to grow, so you it would be wise to accommodate those devices on your websites.

To give you an example of how much leverage you can gain on the Internet, I have a 9 year old Google AdWords account that I set up in 2007 for one of my other real estate niches where I sell investment cash flow properties to investors all around the world.

When I set the account up, I made several ads and had a total of around 1,500 keywords. I set the budget low and placed low bids on the long-tail keywords. From 2007 to 2014 I spent a total of $4,800 with that account. The investment buyers I sourced from that traffic were responsible for over $2,500,000 in flip revenues. That is a very high rate of return on the marketing expense.

Google AdWords works - The key is to do extensive research on keyword analysis.

Basic Digital System for this Niche

The purpose of this is for the motivated sellers that are scared to call you at first, so having the web input form helps overcome that and when they see you are real and local then they open up a little.

It is also very important to not really use a lot of hype phrases-like ads " *CASH FOR HOMES NOW*" " *WE BUY HOMES CASH FASSSST!!*'

The reason being, many of the sleeper deals are elderly citizens that are very distrustful of this kind of marketing. Be creative and test alternative headlines or scripting. This has only been my experience, you can still get deals with the same old marketing words, but I noticed I get more response rates when I use other more creative headlines.

Have a Seller funnel page where they input their property info and have the option of calling you too. Place a few low-budget local ads in your AdWords account

Place a few low budget Facebook ads in your local market for sellers. Use an autoresponder like MailChimp or AWeber for rapid follow up, always include your direct phone # so they can call you if they have the courage. If you know your market you can make an offer right over the phone.

MLS and Broker Relationships

A great way for long term deal flow. Example: I established relationships with the local REO brokers where I live and it has paid off tremendously. Once you have a relationship, they will often give you "pocket listings" whereby you get the chance to make an offer before it actually hits the public MLS as active. It's a little un-ethical according to most people, but when you are the buyer you have significant leverage.

Don't ever back out of a deal without a really good reason, if you do that the broker/agent will most likely not give you a pocket listing again. I've had to close on deals I changed my mind about because I didn't want to damage the broker relation. It sucks but I knew that this broker would get GREAT deals in the future, so I didn't want to jeopardize that.

Newspaper Ads

People still read newspapers, especially the elderly property owners. Print ads have come way down in price. My investor buddy in Cleveland, Mike Alder, uses this strategy to get super cheap deals.

He has no competition because most new investors stopped placing print ads a long time ago. Most 65+ homeowners do not go on the Internet; they still read the newspaper, so you can get great leads this way that the competition will never get.

How to Automate For Simple Cash Flow

Use Digital Marketing Technologies on a Small Scale

What I use to source deals by default on the Internet

- Simple and small Google / Facebook ad accounts (Sellers)
- Monthly expenditure no more than $150 to $250. (sellers)
- Weekly email blast to my cash investor email list (Buyers)
- FREE postings to Facebook real estate groups locally. Use a personal account to avoid getting banned by FB. Don't post more than 5 groups per day. (Sellers)

- Sometimes I network with financial professionals to do an email ad to their databases. Can cost anywhere from $500 to $2000 per email blast. But, once again, one deal can yield $10,000 to $20,000 in profit. I only use this for finding motivated sellers.

I use a couple different form funnel/squeeze pages whereby the seller fills out super brief information; Such as: Name, Email, Phone number and basic property info. The rest of my angle is stated in the autoresponder.

Autoresponders

Seller immediately gets an email from me describing in full honesty with no hype what I do and how I can help. I disclose my address, business name, corporation, phone number, cellular, etc. My goal is to get trust established right away because there are so many fake swindlers out there that ruin it for everyone else. You especially have to do this with the elderly owners. They usually call in my experience. If they entered their phone number on the portal page call them as soon as possible.

Keep It Simple – It's A Marketing Numbers Game

Keep everything simple and stress-free. Get really good at one or two marketing techniques. Keep all ends of this little business fully operational. It is proven and works.

In recap, the goal is to spend about 2 hours per day or less attracting and analyzing bargain deals in hot local markets that you can sell lightning fast for a $10,000 to $30,000 profit by simply placing it on the MLS or notifying your local list of cash rehabbers, **you have to get good at marketing; besides, any business you do you will have to be an expert in marketing, this is a fact.**

You only have to automate the seller lead management aspect, because the buyers are already there waiting for you! You should be able to automate a net profit of $150,000 per year with only 10 hours a week.

How To Enhance Your Wholesale Profits

All of the information below and more are covered in much greater detail in the total LiquidProfits Real Estate Course. All of it is real life scenarios, media and strategies I used in Cleveland and Phoenix personally and covers ALL of my wholesale flipping niche strategies that I use even going into 2018.

Type of Neighborhood

You want to pick a neighborhood in your city that is urban/semi-urban, trendy, hipster or borderline hipster. A location where millennial and middle age home-owners are looking to purchase. In my market this would be Lakewood, Kamms corner, Ohio City, Tremont, Downtown, Coventry area of Cleveland Heights.

It can also be a suburb that has an annual positive net migratory population trend. There is a market of people, although dwindling, that are looking to move out of city areas and into suburbia.

However, the new trend is homeowners looking to move back into the city, but decent areas where there is already a trend occurring, every city has these areas.

Establish A "Farm"

I'm sure you've heard of this technique before but thought it sounded stupid?

IT IS A GOLDMINE!

Farming a zip code is what will ensure you make money with very little effort. You can farm your area using basic techniques such as; Constant direct mail, driving around looking for suspect homes (again this works, it has paid off many times for many years). Direct mail works great if used consistently. I always get a deal or 2 from 1 mailing, which is usually only 500 to 1,500 letters.

Facebook and Google AdWords are the best new digital tools to use for farming areas too. Facebook allows to you really fine tune your cheap ads geographically and google can do local search query ads only if you choose that option in your Adwords account.

- Use direct mail to attract leads.
- Use Internet technologies to automate the process for attracting Seller leads.

- Scan MLS daily in your farm zone (or use Realtor.com).
- Drive your farm couple times a week or at least once a week.

It's simple and 80/20, you will become an EXPERT in your farm because you are limiting yourself to one or 2 areas and that is all that is needed to pull $100k to $200k in net profits a year from it, be a big fish in a small pond.

Cash Is Necessary

You must have access to cash to buy. If you don't have cash, there is an enormous amount of private wealth in every city looking for someone like you to invest it for a fair rate of return. You are going to be buying property at super low price points so your benefit to getting your offers accepted is the fast close for cash strategy. In a Sellers market, creative-type offers on homes are mostly rejected because there are too many other buyers with cash or solid financing lined up. This makes your offer seem worthless to a seller.

In my experienced humble opinion, you need to buy with cash because; sellers are giving up equity for that. Sorry if you are a super strong believer in the creative real estate methods, I am not saying anything negative or that they don't work, but to get great deals with no stress, have cash lined up, whether it's yours or a partner, or a line of credit or a private lender. It's just so much simpler, it's how I started back in the early 2000's in Cleveland, I used a private lender @ 10% which was a high rate at that time.

You need to waive inspections.

Sellers are giving you a discount; they won't entertain someone doing a professional home inspection. You can do walk-through inspections when you look at it yourself though, which is why you must know what to look for in bargain real estate so that you don't buy a major loser.

Partners

I don't recommend taking on equity partners for wholesale flips. The margins will be too low. I recommend finding a debt investor that will be happy with a 10% -15% simple interest return or a flat fee point charge, like $2,000 per deal.

You can find these private investors by searching your county recorder's office for recent private mortgage filings. Most likely those investors just lent someone a private loan and would be interested in working with you too. Every city has them. Most counties have an online database so this is merely a search task using their database.

Your Ideal Seller (Don't Bother With the Rest)

The seller you will be focusing on, other than REO, is going to be someone that wants out now. The timing is perfect and somehow your letter or marketing resonated with him/her at the right time.

They will call you, they will want to talk to you NOW, and they are not going to insult or belittle you because you are the solution to their immediate problem. They will meet you at the house and be willing to do a deal on the spot.

You will make a cash offer you are embarrassed about (one of my core requirements), and they will call you that night to accept it. You won't believe it, and you will think this can only happen once or was a chance encounter or luck. It's not, it can be systematized.

You aren't going to understand how you got such a great deal in a great area. You may think this cannot happen again but I assure you it can and will if you keep farming your farm area and stay consistent with the marketing.

How Do You Find These Types of Motivated Sellers in Hot Local Markets?

This is the hard part for most people to understand. It has a lot to do with timing, you being on the Seller's mind at the right time and being very alert of your flip farm zone and constantly working it at least 5-10 hours a week.

It really is just that simple, there is no magic.

CHAPTER 3

WHY HOT MARKETS?

"Sleeper Deals"

I define a sleeper deal as a distress property that is off-market and not known by anyone in the flipping community YET, in a limbo state due to the owners not caring or in some form of distress or complacency. They need someone like you to come along and show them what to do (Sell low to you for cash).

They typically don't last long as someone will eventually come along, or they decide to list with an agent (Too late).

In hot areas you want to focus on NON-MLS listed homes as much as possible to stay away from the competition. This is your golden spot. When you get these deals, your competition will not understand how you got the deal.

You will have an incredible advantage over competitors because; they are all looking at MLS and Sheriff Sale / Trustee Sales.

Driving your farm, sending 100 letters (click2mail.com) a week and doing some online ads is way too much work for most people, even though it can be done in 1 hour a day and cost less than $5,000 per year! Would you spend $5,000 per year to make $200,000+per year?

So What Are Sleeper Deals In Hot Areas?

- Estates in transitions, squabbling heirs and/or attorneys
- Tax delinquent houses owned by the elderly free and clear
- Vacant houses with no future direction
- Out of town owners not aware of the Market cycle
- Motivated small bank-seller ready to do a price reduction (MLS)
- New REO listing about to come onto the market (Pocket listing) with a Broker you have a relationship with.

The one common denominator I must state for this niche is that most of these sellers are going to be over age 60 with health problems and confused as what to do with the house. They may have trust issues with Agents and Buyers. So if you are good with talking to seniors, then this is even better.

If you spotted a new foreclosure that is bank owned and about to be listed with a local REO broker, you can get to them before it's listed and see if they will let you make an offer right out the door. I have gotten many great deals this way, but this takes trust to establish because it is regarded as unethical and they don't know if you are a "snitch" or "checker" from the State.

The best old method by far is direct mail campaigns to senior property owners in tax foreclosure or default, or where it is vacant just sitting there with no direction. Estates are good too but can take a while to close if heirs are involved and bureaucratic attorneys.

Often these are heirs that don't know what to do or are fighting over assets among other siblings. Eventually you will find one that likes your proposal and is exactly what they want in that moment (Timing) and will agree to your low cash offer. Most of the time these houses are off the MLS, so the general public has no idea.

According to the trends I see developing in various cities; tax defaults/foreclosures and estate sales are the new wave of distress properties. Mortgage foreclosures have reduced significantly in the past few years, but that doesn't mean that people defaulting on their mortgages has diminished; the banks are just following the Federal Reserve's mandate regarding their distressed asset management policies. There is a lot of speculation as to why they do this, most believe it is to falsely inflate the real estate markets, which seems to be working. No one really knows what the Central Banks and Federal Reserve are really up to, probably not anything that is in the Public's best interest, though.

CHAPTER 4

HOW TO FIND HIDDEN DEALS IN HOT AREAS

Driving is #1

I cannot stress this. You will get really good at intuitively knowing a house that you need to look up. It will have subtle clues. No blinds, paper notice or posting on the front window, unkempt lawn, just a "sixth sense". You will get really good because you are confined to a farm and will know the streets and properties very well.

Constant Direct Mail

One of my favorite methods that VERY few investors do consistently anymore is direct mail. I get my lists for free from the county auditors department through their Linux server. Not all County's provide this service though. I also sometimes use CoreLogic for areas where they won't give it to me for free. CoreLogic is not cheap. I tried using MLS software generated property lists but find they are incredibly inaccurate.

Broker Relations

Find out who gets the REO listings and go from there. Track foreclosures that were recently bought by the bank, and will eventually become a MLS listing. Make sure you are there first with your best offer. Sometimes these are called "pocket listings" if you're lucky.

Google AdWords

Set up one small account with a small funnel page for seller leads. I am now spending under $2,000 per year for Google seller lead ads; Small and simple. The ROI is incredible.

Facebook Ads

Set up a business page and linked seller portal page. I place cheap $5 a day FB ads that drive local targeted traffic, it's not a lot but I get some deals from it, and they are growing, possible may exceed AdWords in the near future. <u>I spend less on FB than on Google because I get more **serious** Buyers from Google.</u>

When doing the free FB group postings be careful not to get banned. Use your personal FB account for group postings. **Warning**: It is very easy to get banned or locked out on FB, be very conservative!

Attorneys and Estates

It works! They are always involved in estates. If they can ethically bypass a real estate agent they will. I establish relations in person from post cards. Many will call you out of the blue looking for a fast cash close when you least expect it be ready for that from attorneys, they can be very impatient when they want something now.

When they have a deal that they are asking too much on or it is not the right type of deal for you, don't lie to them or blow them off, be real upfront and honest, attorneys respect that, they know that you are a businessman/woman and will understand if you are not able to make money on the deal, then you won't buy it. Their time is very valuable.

Actual Deals

<u>Lakewood, Ohio</u>

I found this vacant home through a professional network connection - insurance. I simply asked an agent if he knew of anyone that wants to sell a house during a casual conversation. He said yes and called his client and asked if she would sell.

Deal Components:

This owner was elderly and in a state of indecision/no direction with house. It was vacant because they moved out 1 year prior. The husband had medical problems and they needed someone to come along and offer to take the problem away with a fast cash closing.

My insurance agent called and put the option of a fast sale in front of her. Plus he already had trust with her. I gave my agent a referral fee and bought the house for an unheard of amount; $16,000 in a hot market on a NICE street. This is a $180,000 house - after repairs. I quickly flipped the house to a cash rehabber from MLS for $60,000. This really upset the investor local community because they do not understand how I purchased so low.

Sourced: Financial Network Referral
Net Profit: $44,000
Expenses: 1 lockbox
Hours worked: 1-2 hours

<u>Lakewood, Ohio</u>

I found this vacant house by driving around a very desirable area. It was cold and snowy out that day. I noticed a sticker on the window, got out and looked at it, and it was a code violation notice from the city. I could also tell it was vacant from the street because there were no blinds on any of the windows/ I looked up the info when I got home and discovered the following:

The bank recently abandoned the $80,000 mortgage

They simply released it, unbeknownst to the owner. I used see this often during the housing crash. It costs the bank more to foreclose than it would to just walk away from a foreclosure. Seems unbelievable but I have bought properties like this on multiple occasions.

The property had code violations from City.

It had 2 tax liens sold at auction, so they were attached and had to be paid off at value plus 18% interest. Records revealed that the total tax lien payoff came to $29,000. This means I could get a $150,000 house for only $29,000.

Components:

I looked up the owner, had to do some skip tracing but found her living with her daughter in an apartment tower in an adjacent city. I sent her a letter stating that I would take this burden off her hands, but I did not state how much I would pay,. I also did not mention the mortgage abandonment.

She called me a week later and was an 80-year old woman that said she was having strokes over this house. She said I could have it for free. We had an hour-long conversation, she was somewhat skeptical at first but I just kept our conversation simple and real honest, and no hype. I remained DETACHED. Three weeks later I bought it for $29,000, basically the tax payoffs. The owners were willing to give it to me for free!

I showed a young Realtor friend the house and he was shell-shocked with disbelief and could not understand how I bought this so low (typical SleeperDeal reaction!), he made me a cash offer for himself right there on the spot of $41,000. Once again, no buyer marketing.

Note: I could have sold it for $60,000 on MLS! But my Realtor buddy wanted the house so bad, and I needed his help with making a lot of low-ball agency offers so I gave him the equity. He remodeled the entire house and it recently appraised for $195,000 (March of 2018).

Sourced:	Driving Reconnaissance
Net Profit:	$11,000
Hours worked:	1.5

Cleveland, Ohio

This was a MLS sourced property believe it or not, but I had bought several properties from this bank in the past, they recognized my name as a real serious closer so that had some influence and I also acted VERY FAST and had a good agent. Bottom line though, I was alerted to the picture-less listing as soon as it went online, and made an offer within the first 2 hours. I knew the area very well (farm) and drove by it and called my local agent for an emergency offer. This was simply good timing, beating the lazy competition to it. I ended up securing it for $20,000 less than asking. I was simply at the right place at the right time.

Deal Components:

- Saturday bank foreclosure
- Asset manager was working on a Saturday
- Most people were watching the ball game
- Fast action made all the difference; made an all low offer with no contingencies.

I relisted the property on discount MLS for $20k over what I paid, it went under contract within 5 days to a cash buyer owner-occupant. This house needed $40,000 in repairs. It is worth over $155,000 after repairs.

Sourced: MLS REO
Net Profit: $18,000
Hours worked: 45 minutes

Selling Fast For Cash Profits In A Hot Area

"Velocity is important in wholesale real estate flipping - the last thing you want is holding costs."

This is the easy part. I like to get professional sunny pics from a photographer and place it on the MLS with a discount service where I pay 3.75% commission max. I used to use www.MLSMyHome.com before I established a broker relation that does this for me now. I generally go under contract within a week. The MLS and all of the syndicated networks like Zillow and Realtor.com are your friend in a hot market. All buyers are looking at it on their smart phone and tablets. They get email alerts every day; You will have a rapid response to your flip!

Two of the recent deals I showed you were so great that I didn't even have to list on the MLS, I simply told one rehabber about it and he quickly bought it, and I told a young agent about the other one and he snapped it up for himself to rehab and live in. All paid cash.

In addition to MLS, I always recommend you have a direct mail campaign send out to the area's list of recent cash buyers of property. This information is free from your county auditor. Make a letter or card that is honest and to the point. Don't be too promotional. Seasoned investors can see right through hype. They know the areas too.

Compile and update your list every month. Cash buyers only, preferable ones with different tax mailing addresses (rehabbers or landlords). I would not use 3rd party software to do this mailing for you. If you really get great deals, one investor could be a repeat buyer for many years and deals.

I cannot tell you how many times I get cheap postcards from other investors that all say the same thing (A script they got from a real estate course) for a property I don't even own anymore. What always baffled me was that they would spend $5,000 to $15,000 on coaching and software but not even have the mental creativity to adjust the redundant postcard script.

" We are THE Premier real estate Investment Company in the whole area, We get great deals and want to place you on our VIP Wholesale buyers' list. Call today!"

- Lists an out of state phone number.
- Has a local mailing address.

Even my investors I sell to won't call these postcards - they call me for more homes.

Do Not Do

Buy Houses With Deed Restrictions

If you are buying REO property and you get a HUD, Fannie or Freddie home, they will have a 90-day deed restriction, you cannot sell for 90 days.

Buyers with Traditional Home Inspection Clauses

Often used by hesitant buyers to have a way out. If it is an owner-occupant this is ok, but for rehabbers they should know better and know what they are getting into. I would not let a rehabber put this clause in your sales contract.

Take on Mega-Repairs

That's OK rehabbers love them, as long as they are not major structural problems, or you didn't over pay for the property.

Cash Flow Rentals

When there are non-paying squatting tenants in the house, use a lawyer to file an eviction to get them out. Where I live the process takes about a month. Sometimes just offering cash for keys is the best way to get them to move. You can also pass this burden onto the cash buyer.

MLS Mistakes

Do not list your home, accept a skeptical offer from an excited buyer with questionable proof of funds letter or financing contingencies, and have it come back on the market more than once, this will stigmatize your house as something to avoid, because most buyers will start to think that something is wrong with it, and not even bother with it (house stigma).

Get Greedy or Indecisive

You will get such great deals you will want to rehab them and make the most profit! (Often $50,000 to $100,000). If you have the skills and contacts that's great, of course. But if you are strictly wholesale driven, don't do it. If you have a low tolerance for risk definitely do not do it! Big rehabs always go as NOT expected.

Settle For the Wrong Buyer

If you get an un-questionable offer with not so great terms or price, DON'T SETTLE. In hot areas, the next ideal buyer is right in line, and another one after that.

Why This Niche Will Grow

The new housing distress wave is tax defaults/sold tax lien property and estates, especially in the elderly (65+). This is a huge opportunity; many of these homes are in hot neighborhoods of major cities and smaller cities.

<u>**Most investors are not looking for and reaching out to these HIDDEN deals. They are scouring the MLS and foreclosure Auctions/Trustee Sales and Auction websites**</u>.

You can develop one "farm" or have multiple ones in your region.

Your only strategy will be wholesale flipping. 90% of your competition is lazy, so you have a major advantage. When I say lazy I mean that they are not using their creative marketing powers to find these hidden deals that you are. Most of your buyers in a hot area will pay cash, even owner - occupants.

Obstacles

One of the biggest mental blocks investors have is that they won't be able to find a grand slam deal in these hot areas. I assure you they are there. When you LEAST expect it, you get a call from one of your letters, ads or you drive by a house that seems suspicious, and you send a letter to the owner, and they call you, and this is just how it works, It is not magical, it's being consistent and not giving up. Real estate has cycles and your local market will become a Buyers' market again too, although not all Buyers' markets are similar in price.

"This is just one niche of the wholesaling flipping businesses, there are many more to choose from"

For more information on real estate investing, contact me below.

ValleyWide Real Estate Investments, LLC
ValleyWideInvestments.com
(216) 220-7027

www.ingramcontent.com/pod-product-compliance
Lightning Source LLC
Chambersburg PA
CBHW071438220526
45469CB00004B/1578